CodeWell Academy() and R.M.Z.

present:

Artificial Intelligence
Made Easy, w/ Ruby Programming

2nd Edition

*Learn to Create your * Problem Solving * Algorithms! TODAY! w/ Machine Learning & Data Structures*

Artificial Intelligence Series

INCLUDES BONUS: Easiest Way to Learn Ruby

Table of Contents

4

Preface: RUBY as Artificial Intelligence

========================== ======

How you'll progress through this book

The goal of this book is to expand your programming skills onto a new paradigm - namely, the realm of artificial intelligence. You may be a skilled programmer hoping to learn new skills, or someone new to programming, or even both. No matter what your programming skill level is, we hope you find some intriguing information within these pages.

You'll see first-hand how algorithm procedures within AI make decisions and generate answers, given sets of data.

First, we'll go over Constraint Satisfaction. Ever had schedule a night out with friends, but had to consider their availability throughout a day? Of course, you'd ask what times they're available. Now, try scheduling a meeting with thousands of people. That'll be quite hard to do alone, wouldn't it?

Next, we'll go over Logic-Based Systems. Here, we make an entire logic-based system with interconnected statements, where one logical fact affects another. Once we have the system in place, we can create procedures - which AI will eventually use - to check, analyze, and diagnose the system to see if it runs as intended.

Then, we'll go over perhaps one of the most important algorithms in artificial intelligence - the Search Algorithm. We'll analyze its procedure carefully, giving you a great opportunity to apply it step-by-step. Afterwards, we'll discuss its variants, including their strengths, weaknesses, and best applications. You'll discover the subtle little variances in the algorithm that make a tremendous impact on its procedure - and results.

In essence, Search Algorithms can be an artificial intelligence agent's model of thought, generating a process to achieve a goal given the resources it has.

To give you an idea of how powerful search algorithms can be, you can use them not just to search your records, but to to solve puzzles and riddles for you.

A Quick Start

If all this sounds intimidating to you, don't worry.

Included is a quick kit to cover Basic Ruby Programming. You'll find what you need to get a good start in programming Ruby. Then, you'll be prepared to use the many tools and components of AI throughout the book.

Introduction

==== ==== ==== ==== ====

Logic. Rationality. Reasoning. Thought. Analysis. Calculation. Decision-making.

All this is within the mind of a human being, correct? Humanity has been blessed with the ability to think and act so intelligently.

Then came Machine. Humanity has also blessed it the gift of intelligence.

And in today's world, you can see firsthand what an intelligent mind can do for you; carry a conversation, give you directions to a certain location, play a video game as an opponent, and so on.

In essence, only our imaginations will limit us from what's truly possible

An Artificial Intelligence Agent

In terms of Artificial Intelligence, an agent can be anything that, given an environment to focus on, can think intelligently and act independently. It can continue observing and learning through experience. It can calculate and independently decide the best course of action, whether it has perfect knowledge of the situation or just a part of it. It can also take note and adapt to a changing environment.

So you might wonder, how has mankind ever developed something so complex?

Well, it's not as complex as you think.

If you understand the process of how a computer can observe, learn, and expand its knowledge - and how it can take all this information and come up with an ideal solution or decision - then an artificially created mind won't be as complex as you think.

Sometimes, it can take as little as a few lines of code to have a computer come up with solutions for you. Sometimes it can take hundreds. Sometimes, thousands.

Chapter 1: Algorithms: The Essentials

==== ==== ==== ==== ====

In essence, how an AI agent will contemplate, process, rationalize, apply logic, & ultimately generate solutions will mainly be through the use of algorithms.

If you're new to programming, don't be intimidated. An algorithm is essentially a procedure to handle data. As long as you understand how a certain algorithm processes its data, you'll be fine.

Algorithm Traits

First, you'll want your algorithms to satisfy four key factors:

- Completeness

- Optimization

- Time Complexity

- Space Complexity

Now we'll go through each of these and explain them all. Afterwards, you'll explore some algorithm ideas and determine how they fit in to each of these factors.

Completeness

If an algorithm is guaranteed to find at least one existing solution or conclusion within a certain time frame, we can say that an algorithm is complete.

Optimization

If an algorithm finds a solution and guarantees that it is the optimal one, then that algorithm is considered optimal.

Time Complexity

For an algorithm, this is an expression for the longest possible time it will take to complete. In other words, the worst-case scenario when it runs and finds a suitable solution.

Space Complexity

This expression is similar to Time Complexity, but instead it represents the maximum amount of memory the algorithm may use in order to find a solution. This is also considered the worst-case scenario.

Your Ideal Algorithm

After discussing the traits your algorithm can have, you'll get an idea in what to look for when creating an AI algorithm. You want to design yours to find at least one solution (completeness), and the best solution it can create given data it has (optimization) while using up as little computational effort as you can (Time & Space Complexity)

Chapter 1.1: Problem-Solving AI

==== ==== ==== ==== ====

An AI agent will have its goals and ideal preferences. Now it just needs to find a way to get to them. It needs to search and create a way to achieve them.

How would it do this? First, it will create a set of options. Then, it will check to see which options will lead to a solution. And based on the goals or preferences we've defined, we could figure out which options will ultimately lead to the best solution. And just to be sure that it works, you can also run test cases for your algorithm as well.

Let's take a look at a self-driving taxi as an example. To get from its current place to its destination (assuming it's driving across the downtown portion of a large city) it will analyze which route is the fastest. For each intersection it will potentially approach, it can proceed or turn left or right depending on the rules of the road. Afterwards, it may reach another intersection, and it will have to choose between proceeding or turning left or right.

Eventually, for each possible path it assesses, it might or might not reach the destination. For the paths that do, your AI agent will use one of them as the route to follow. Problem solved!

```
[ Current Location ]
|
|————[Turn Left]—-[Turn Left] ...
|                 |————-[ Turn Right] ... [ Reached Dest'n ]
|                 '————-[ Proceed ] ...
|
|————[Turn Right]—-[Turn Left] ...
|                 |————-[ Turn Right] ... [ Reached Dest'n ]
|                 '————-[ Proceed ] ...
|
|                 |————-[ Turn Right] ...
|                 '————-[ Proceed ] ...
'————[Proceed]—-[Turn Left] ...
```

In the next few pages, we'll try out some procedures and algorithms that generate solutions for you. Each will have different data models and approaches, depending on the goals and preferences you want.

RUBY 01a: using AI to Solve Complex Time Scheduling

========================== ======

Imagine 5 of your friends trying to get together and have fun somewhere.

It might sound simple at first, but it can become far more complicated than you think.

What if one of your friends has work at certain times? What if another friend has school? What if he/she has a prior engagement? Soccer practice? Dance classes? Study time? Sure, you can all get together and have fun. However, it has to be at a time when EVERYONE is available.

So, given each friend you have, you need to lay out their time schedules, then cross out times that they're busy. Afterwards, if there is some common available time among all your friends, everyone says they're available, then you and your friends have fun.

Let's have another example.

How do you think a 32-team Sports League will schedule games throughout a year? For all 32 teams, they each need to match up with up to one other team to schedule a game. Each team needs a certain amount of games scheduled in a season of, say, 6 months. There can only be a certain number of games in a single week and there needs to be enough time to travel between cities to have a game.

These are times when a Scheduling Algorithm can help. It will take all members' availabilities and time constraints, then generate a viable solution. For scheduling, it can tell you what times of the day is everyone available. For large-scale implementations, it can be used to schedule sports league match-ups, schedule exams for tens of thousands of college students, and more.

A very simple and easy algorithm to start with is the Generate-and-Test algorithm.

The next chapters will show you the Algorithm and guide you through its procedure...

RUBY 01b: The Generate-And-Test General Algorithm

For the procedure below, select an IDE of your choice. You may also use online IDE's such as rextester.com, ideone.com, or codepad.org.

========================== ======

This is the generalized algorithm, including the explanatory comments:

INPUT:
- any number of Lists
- at least one Goal Function (must return a Boolean)
- any number of Constraint Functions (each must return a Boolean)
OUTPUT: - (optional; select any output type)
EFFECT: - For all possible combinations of each list,
check to see if it's the goal combination,
while checking if it satisfies the constraints.

```
def generateAndTest(list1, list2, ... listN, goal1(), ..
goalN(), cons1(), ... consN() )
list1.each do |a|
  list2.each do |b|

    ...
        listN.each do |n|
          if goal1(a,b, ..., n) and ... goalN(a,b, ..., n)
                and cons1(a,b, ..., n) and ... consN(a,b, ...,
n)
              ## === Solution Results are Here
              ## Post Code with what you want to do
              ## ===
            end
          end

      ...
    end
end
```

The next chapters will show you, step-by-step, how to build this algorithm.

RUBY 01c: The Procedure: Schedule Solvers

For the procedure below, select an IDE of your choice. You may also use online IDE's such as <u>rextester.com</u>, <u>ideone.com</u>, or <u>codepad.org</u>.

============================ ======

Step 1: Your Friends, and their Hours

For each one of your friends, create a Global Variable and set it to an Array. Within the array, set your values from 0 to 23. We'll use integers to represent all 24 hours of a 24-hour clock. For simplicity's sake, we'll only use a single day of the week. If you want, you also have the option to set your integer hours using four digits to include minutes, such as 1330 (1:30 pm) or 1745 (5:45 pm).

For our example, let's say your friends are Anna, Betty, Cara, and Donna. We'll include the integers to represent the 24-hour clock. However, we skip hours 0-8 because, clearly, everyone needs some good sleeping hours.

Anna = [9, 10, 11,12,13,14,15,16,17,18, 19, 20, 21, 22, 23]
Betty = [9, 10, 11,12,13,14,15,16,17,18, 19, 20, 21, 22, 23]
Cara = [9, 10, 11,12,13,14,15,16,17,18, 19, 20, 21, 22, 23]
Donna = [9, 10, 11,12,13,14,15,16,17,18, 19, 20, 21, 22, 23]

Step 2: The Goal Function

Your goal is to determine which hours are everyone available.

Represent this with a function. There are as many integer inputs as there are friends to schedule. The function outputs True if all the input hours are equal.

```
# Goal 1: Have an hour of the day when EVERYONE is
available to meet
# INPUT: Four Integers, representing Hours
# OUTPUT: Boolean
# EFFECT: return True if all input hours are equal
def g1(a, b, c, d)
    return (a == b and b == c and c == d)
end
```

Step 3: Time Constraints

For each of your friends to schedule, create a function to represent which hours are unavailable. A friend's hours aren't available if he/she is preoccupied by something at that time.

 # Constraint Functions
 # INPUT: an Integer, representing a friend's Hour
 # OUTPUT: Boolean
 # EFFECT: return True if the hour satisfies the time constraints

In our example, we're going to create a bunch of time constraints for each friend. Some have school, work, and other stuff.

```
# Constraint 1: Anna has classes 11am - 1:50pm
def c1(a)
    return (a < 11 or a > 13)
end
```

```
# Constraint 2: Betty has classes noon - 3pm,
# then has dance practice until 4pm
def c2(b)
    return (b < 12 or b >= 16)
end
```

```
# Constraint 3: Cara has work 7pm to 11pm
def c3(c)
    return (c < 19 or c > 23)
end

# Constraint 4: Diana has volunteer hours from 6pm to
8pm,
# and work 8pm to 11pm
def c4(d)
    return (d < 18 or d > 22)
end
```

Step 4: The Main Algorithm

We will be using a simple Generate-and-Search Algorithm to solve the Scheduling Problem.

How it works is, for each Hour of Each Friend, the algorithm will check if the combination of hours are valid - based on the Goal and Constraint Functions we made in Step 2 and 3.

To make this Algorithm, create a series of iteration loops within iteration loops, as shown below, for all your friends to schedule.

At the very centre of your procedure, make an IF statement that includes ALL your goal functions and constraints.

If they all return true, you have a solution!

```
# Main Algorithm: Generate and Search
Anna.each do |v|
  Betty.each do |w|
    Cara.each do |x|
      Donna.each do |y|
        if g1(v, w, x, y) and c1(v) and c2(w) and c3(x) and c4(y)
          ## === Solution Results are Here
          puts "Anna, Betty, Cara, and Diana can hang out at: " + v.to_s + ":00"
          ## ===
        end
      end
    end
  end
end
```

If you use ALL the example code in the steps above and compile/run, here's what it should say:

Anna, Betty, Cara, and Diana can hang out at: 9:00

Anna, Betty, Cara, and Diana can hang out at: 10:00

Anna, Betty, Cara, and Diana can hang out at: 16:00

Anna, Betty, Cara, and Diana can hang out at: 17:00

Computing Effort: Generate-and-Test

This procedure will create a LOT of hour combinations to check. Roughly, it's the number of hours per friend, to the power of how many friends to schedule:

(# of hours) ^ (# of friends)

In our example, we have hours 9 to 23, so that's 15 hours per friend. We have four friends. So that's $15^4 = 50625$ possible hour combinations to check. Don't worry; we're just very lucky that a computer can solve this for us.

RUBY 01d: Schedule Solvers, Faster Version

For the procedure below, select an IDE of your choice. You may also use online IDE's such as <u>rextester.com</u>, <u>ideone.com</u>, or <u>codepad.org</u>.

========================= ======

If you think 50625 combinations is a lot to process, it really is. Sometimes, even for the computer systems themselves.

But what if I told you that there's probably another way?

And what if there's a chance it can solve the schedule with less effort?

In this alternate version, we remove each friend's unavailable hours first, and then we generate a solution.

Steps 1 & 2:

These steps don't change. They follow the same code from the original version.

Step 3: Time Constraints

Here, we've modified the Constraint Functionality.

Notice how they're no longer functions, but direct procedural code to be carried out. Each friend's unavailable hours are pushed into an array, which is used to purge that friend's hours until only the available hours are there.

But you may be thinking, why don't we just delete the item right away? It's because once the number has been deleted, the items in the array after it are shifted over. Once the iteration moves on to the next item, it skips an item.

```
# Constraint Procedures
# Constraint 1: Anna has classes 11am - 1:50pm
delList = []
  $Anna.each do |a|
    if (a >= 11 and a < 14)
      delList.push(a)
    end
  end
## (Delete ALL of Anna's unavailable hours)
delList.each do |z|
  $Anna.delete(z)
end
```

```
# Constraint 2: Betty has classes noon - 3pm,
# then has dance practice until 4pm
delList = []
$Betty.each do |b|
   if (b >= 12 and b < 16)
     delList.push(b)
   end
end

## (Delete ALL of Betty's unavailable hours)
delList.each do |z|
   $Betty.delete(z)
end
# Constraint 3: Cara has work 7pm to 11pm
delList = []
$Cara.each do |c|
   if (c >= 19 and c <= 23)
     delList.push(c)
   end
end
## (Delete ALL of Cara's unavailable hours)
delList.each do |z|
   $Cara.delete(z)
end
```

```
# Constraint 4: Donna has volunteer hours from 6pm to
8pm,
# and work 8pm to 11pm
delList = []
$Donna.each do |d|
  if (d >= 18 and d <= 22)
    delList.push(d)
  end
end
## (Delete ALL of Donna's unavailable hours)
delList.each do |z|
  $Donna.delete(z)
end
```

Just to check if it works, these lines print each friend's hours:

```
puts "Hours Free (after Unavailable Hours Removed):"
print "Anna: "; $Anna.each do |a|; print a, ", "; end;
print "\n";
print "Betty: "; $Betty.each do |a|; print a, ", "; end;
print "\n";
print "Cara: "; $Cara.each do |a|; print a, ", "; end; print
"\n";
print "Donna: "; $Donna.each do |a|; print a, ", "; end;
print "\n";
puts ""
```

Afterwards, this should be the output:

Hours Free (after Unavailable Hours Removed):

Anna: 9, 10, 14, 15, 16, 17, 18, 19, 20, 21, 22, 23,

Betty: 9, 10, 11, 16, 17, 18, 19, 20, 21, 22, 23,

Cara: 9, 10, 11, 12, 13, 14, 15, 16, 17, 18,

Donna: 9, 10, 11, 12, 13, 14, 15, 16, 17, 23,

Step 4: The Main Algorithm

What's different between this alternate algorithm and the original one is the IF statement in the middle. Since the constraints aren't functions anymore and your friends' hours had their unavailable hours removed, you only need to have the goal function:

```
# Main Algorithm: Generate and Search
$Anna.each do |v|
  $Betty.each do |w|
    $Cara.each do |x|
      $Donna.each do |y|
        if g1(v, w, x, y)
          ## === Solution Results are Here
          puts "Anna, Betty, Cara, and Donna can hang
out at: " + v.to_s + ":00"
          ## ===
        end
      end
    end
  end
end
```

If you run the code overall, they'll generate the same hours available: 9 & 10 am; and 4 & 5 pm (16:00 and 17:00, respectively).

Computing Effort: Generate-and-Test

The original list had 50625 hour combinations to check.

In this alternate version - after all unavailable hours were removed - we have a total of 12 x 11 x 10 x 10 = 13200 versions to check.

The Constraint procedures didn't take much effort either. Each friend's array of hours were only iterated through at least twice; once to check for unavailable hours, and twice or more to remove them.

Between both versions, the difference was tens of thousands of combinations.

If it doesn't seem like much now, if this procedure were to check HUNDREDS or THOUSANDS of people - and their available hours - then different versions of the procedure can have HUGE differences in their efforts spent.

So always remember: when you design algorithms of any sort, you have to take the procedure times and memory space into account. If there's a more efficient procedure, use it.

Chapter 2: Logic & Reasoning

==== ==== ==== ==== ====

Logic and AI?

Boolean, or "True/False" logic is widely used in the field of Artificial Intelligence. It is essentially working with a collection of facts and statements that are either true or false.

Think of the implementations for AI. You can use logic-based programming to have an AI agent make better decisions based on certain conditions. Further, you can have an AI agent diagnose technical problems, and even have AI agents take actions for you - such as fetch coffee (if the robot meets certain conditions, that is).

Why use Logic?

Perhaps the most compelling reason is how simple, easy, and natural it is to express facts and statements as true or false. You can have a statement such as "We're having steak dinner tonight", yet it clearly can't be represented by numbers. You can also try assigning variables as strings or objects as such, but that will require more time and effort.

But as a boolean, the statement "We're having steak dinner tonight" will either be True or False. It's that simple; either it's true (we really are having steak dinner tonight) or it's false.

An AI agent can use several true/false statements and combine them in complex ways. And even so, the AI agent will manage the information much more easily. This is because one true statement can lead to another, then another, resulting in a conclusion, decision, or even a course of action for the agent.

Adding more Logic

We can even add more facts and knowledge easily, if needed. There can be one true fact or two. Then two true or false facts lead to another truth. Then another. For example, we can say a true statement such as, "it's sunny outside", then another such as "it's warm outside". These statements can lead to another truth: "It's sunny AND warm outside. Therefore, I will be running for a mile".

If you put the above together into a proposition statement, it would look like so:

"I will be running for a mile" <— "it's sunny outside" AND "it's sunny outside"

And if you use variable labels to represent the above statements, it would look like so:

c <— b AND a

Debugging with Logic

Conversely, you can use logic to explain the root causes of a certain fact. If one statement is true, it can be explained and justified by another fact, then those facts are justified by more facts, and so on. Here's an example: you realize that "the remote control is not turning on the TV." You carefully look at the remote and realize "its batteries are dead". You change the batteries on the remote, try to turn on the TV, and realize that it's still not turning on. You check the TV power cord and realize "it's not plugged in." Okay, you plug it in, try to turn it on again. And this time, it works.

You can have the above as step-by-step logic statements as so:

1) True: "The remote control is NOT turning on the TV."

2) True: "TV power cord is NOT plugged in"

3) True: "Remote batteries are NOT charged"

AND "TV power cord is NOT plugged in"

This procedure is often used for debugging; if you find something that doesn't work, you must go back and examine the inner workings to figure out what's causing it.

How AI analyzes a Logic-Based System

An AI agent can analyze a given system based on whether or not certain conditions are true. Those conditions will lead to other conditions being true or not, then other conditions, and so on.

There are two general procedures to do this. First is a top-down diagnosis, where the procedure will check certain key conditions (most likely topmost statements that affect other conditions), then go through the system to see what results.

The other is a bottom-up diagnosis, where the procedure will check why a certain end condition is or isn't what it should be. This is done by checking what other conditions lead it to be the way it is.

RUBY 02a: Using Logic-Based AI

For the procedure below, select an IDE of your choice. You may also use online IDE's such as rextester.com, ideone.com, or codepad.org.

============================= ======

There are plenty of designs and systems out there. Almost all of them can be represented as logic-based systems - which can be managed by AI systems to diagnose, repair, and analyze. However, in order to have the AI agent manage the system well, its programmer must understand the system very well. The programmer then has to represent the system as a logical code very well.

For example, the electric wiring system in your house can be built using a series of true/false systems. The plugs in the wall, as well as the lights in your room, are all true/false switches that receive their feed from circuit breakers and wiring panels - more sets of true/false switches. This design benefits home developers, as they can trace the main power coming from outside and figure out whether or not electrical power flows to all plugs, lights, and generally anything that needs electricity in the house.

This design also benefits house residents; if a certain light or plug isn't working, the wiring can be traced all the way to the outside source to see where is the electricity getting cut off.

Water Flow In a House Example:

Below is a diagram for water flow for a 1-bedroom suite:

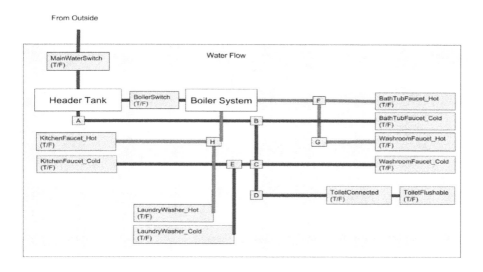

There are taps for the bath tub, washroom sink, and kitchen. The laundry washer can activate for a short time, using some combination of hot and cold water. The toilet has a switch that directs flow to it. The toilet is either flushing or not. Also, there is a switch that either feeds water onto the boiler system or not. There are also taps labelled A to H that stop or allow water flow. And lastly, the Main Water Switch either allows or stops overall water flow into the suite.

Whether or not water will flow from a certain water source will depend on the connections, taps, and switches in the house.

Where are the Switches & Taps?

The first thing you'll want to do is identify which points of water flow in the system above can be toggled on and off.

If you look at the diagram, the switches:

- the pair of hot/cold taps for the bathtub, washroom, and kitchen

- A pair of hot/cold switches laundry washer

- taps labelled A - H

- The Boiler Switch

- The Main Water Switch

These will be boolean taps that are either TRUE, FALSE, or dependent on the true/false state of another switch/tap.

Representing the System as Logical Statements

At this stage, it's best not to code yet. We need to determine how each of the switches feeds water to the next switch - all the way to the end taps that give water to the residents.

We can start with the toilet. House residents use the water by flushing the toilet. We can have a statement such as, "The Toilet can Flush. Therefore, it is connected to the water supply" ; The logic notation is shown below:

ToiletFlushable <- ToiletConnected

We can see that taps A, B, C, and D affect its water flow, as well as the Toilet Connector and the Main Water Switch:

ToiletConnected <- D and C
C <- B and A
A <- MainWaterSwitch

Now we can move on to the rest of the house. For one, both the Kitchen Taps and the Laundry washer depend on taps E and C, which depend on taps B, A, and ultimately, the Main Water Switch. Since both the Kitchen and Laundry use hot water, both of them also depend on tap H.

KitchenTap_Hot <- H
KitchenTap_Cold <- E and C
LaundryWasher_Hot <- H
LaundryWasher_Cold <- E and C
F and H <- BoilerSwitch

The Washroom and Bathtub taps each have a hot and cold tap. The washroom cold tap depends on switch C while the hot tap depends on taps F and G.

WashroomTap_Hot <- F and G
WashroomTap_Cold <- C

And lastly, the bathtub cold water tap depends on tap B releasing water, while the hot water tap depends on tap F to release water.

BathTubTap_Hot <- F
BathTubTap_Cold <- B

If you have everything together, it will look like this:

ToiletFlushable <- ToiletConnected
ToiletConnected <- D and C
C <- B
B <- A
A <- MainWaterSwitch
KitchenTap_Hot <- H
KitchenTap_Cold <- E and C
LaundryWasher_Hot <- H
LaundryWasher_Cold <- E and C

BathTubTap_Hot <- F
BathTubTap_Cold <- B
WashroomTap_Hot <- F and G
WashroomTap_Cold <- C
F and H <- BoilerSwitch

Using AI to Analyze a system

Because we've mapped out the logical links between facts (namely, we now know which taps and switches feed water into what) we can start creating procedure to analyze and diagnose the system.

We'll create both top-down and bottom-up diagnoses for this system, explaining what happens for each one.

The Top-Down Procedure:

Based on how the system was mapped out using boolean logic, we've found five root taps and switches that affect the rest of the water system - the Main Water Switch, the Boiler Switch, and taps D, E, and G. Therefore, a Top-down procedure can determine which water sources within the house are affected.

You can find the Procedure Code in the Appendix section

The Bottom-Up Procedure:

Here, the same five root taps and switches are global variables you can toggle true/false. Then you can run the procedure for one of the water sources in the house to check whether or not water flows through it.

You can also find the Procedure Code in the Appendix section

Chapter 3: Environment Representation for AI

==== ==== ==== ==== ====

Representation Scheme

For an Artificial Intelligence unit to be able to generate data and solutions for you, it will usually need some sort of data source.

And sometimes, this data source depends on the environment: the AI agent will need to determine and observe the environment that it's focused on.

Therefore, the AI agent will need to represent its environment in data. Afterwards, it can process that data with its own algorithms and generate solutions.

RUBY 03a: Environment Models with Ruby

For the procedure below, select an IDE of your choice. You may also use online IDE's such as rextester.com, ideone.com, or codepad.org.

========================= ======

Modelling the Environment

A very crucial element in artificial intelligence is having a code model of its focused environment. For your AI agent to be able to create solutions, it needs to know about its environment and surroundings.

So to model the AI agent's environment, there are two main ways to do so.

First, you can either use the "Traffic Light" principle - have enumerations of the possible states or conditions of the AI agent's focus. This is a very simple representation of an environment.

For example, an AI agent can monitor the traffic lights in your closest intersection and determine which colour the light will be (either Red, Yellow, or Green).

Use this for making very simple interpretations of whatever the AI agent focuses on.

trafficLights = ["Red", "Yellow", "Green"]

Second, you can describe the environment features into detailed data representations. With Object-Oriented Programming, you can simply create class objects about your AI's environment observations - including the many little details as class fields. Use this for more natural, detailed environment observations.

```
class BeachVisit
  def initialize(loc, tide, crowd, temp)
    @location = loc
    @timeDate = Time.new
    @tide = tide
    @crowdSize = crowd
    @temperature = temp
  end

end
```

```
b1 = BeachVisit.new("Santa Monica Beach",
    "high",
    "large",
    "81f")

b2 = BeachVisit.new("Santa Monica Beach",
    "medium",
    "medium",
    "78f")
```

Environment Models using Data Combinations

If you choose your AI agent to describe environments via Object-Oriented Programming, you can also link two objects from different classes. You create a relationship between them, taking note of how they are linked together.

For example, we can take our beach visit objects and link them together with photos:

```
## (assume instances b1 - b25 have been created)
## all beach visits into an array:
allBeachVisits = [b1, b2, b3, b4, b5]
```

(assume instances ph1 - ph7 have been created)
all photos into an array:
allPhotos = [ph1, ph2, ph3, ph4, ph5, ph6, ph7]

// Possible Relation Propositions:
// #1: PhotosTaken
// proposition: return TRUE if photo has been taken during Beach Visit
photoTakenAtVisit(ph1, b3)

// #2: PhotosTaken
// proposition: return TRUE if photo has been taken at Beach Visit location
photoTakenHere(ph3, b5)

RUBY 03b: Creating a Model Environment

For the procedure below, select an IDE of your choice. You may also use online IDE's such as rextester.com, ideone.com, or codepad.org.

=========================== ======

Now let's practice creating environments for our AI to examine. This will all come together later on, as an AI agent will have a chance to explore its environment with its given knowledge and abilities.

Modelling A House

The most simple way you can model an environment is the Traffic Light principle mentioned earlier.

If you model your house in a simple enumeration-type data collection, you might have something similar below:

myHouse = ["livingRoom", "diningRoom", "den", "bathroom1", "bathroom2", "hallway", "bedroom1", "bedroom2", "patio"]

You may also model your house using Object-Oriented Programming. You can represent every room in the house as a Room object.

```
## A Room has:
## - a name
## - adjacent, connected rooms
class Room
  def initialize(name)
    @name = name
    @connected = []
  end

  def add(room)
    @connected.push(room)
  end

  def name
    return @name
  end

  def connected
    return @connected
  end
end
```

To keep things very simple for now, you can model a simple condo in the heart of a thriving downtown core.

```
## Create 5 rooms in a simple condo in the City
kitchen = Room.new("kitchen")
livRM = Room.new("livingRoom")
dineRM = Room.new("diningRoom")
bd = Room.new("bedroom")
wr = Room.new("washroom")


"""
## Connect all rooms as so:
## <-> Washroom <-> Bedroom <-> livingRoom <->
Kitchen <-> DiningRoom <->
"""

kitchen.connected.push(livRM, dineRM)
livRM.connected.push(bd, kitchen)
bd.connected.push(wr, livRM)
wr.connected.push(dineRM, bd)
dineRM.connected.push(kitchen, wr)
```

Whichever way you would like to model your environment is up to you.

Just keep in mind that you will eventually design the AI agent that will correspond to your model environment.

Your Turn

In Ruby (or whichever programming language you want), create a code model of your home based on the to modelling directions above. First, do the "traffic light method" by creating a simple enumeration or array of the rooms in your house.

Then, as Object-Oriented Programming, model your home by having each room represented by Room instances. Then, connect each room accordingly.

Chapter 4: Your AI Knowledge & Abilities

==== ==== ==== ==== ====

Here, we go much more in-depth with an AI agent's knowledge and abilities.

You will have to determine how your AI agent will receive its information - including what abilities it can do.

There are two solutions to this: your AI agent either has all its knowledge given by default; or it will scout/observe/learn its environment and gain information this way. Also, you can choose a combination of both. For now, we focus on Default Knowledge and abilities.

AI Knowledge by Default

Your AI agent can receive, by default, a fixed set of all information it will ever need. If you believe some part of your AI agent's information won't change, you may model your AI agent's information this way.

For example, your AI agent may be a self-driving vehicle. The rules of the road will stay consistent in the long term. Also, its driving patterns and techniques will stay consistent too. The road maps will also stay consistent.

Therefore, your self-driving vehicle can navigate its way through a city and make its way from two points.

AI Knowledge by Learning

Your AI agent can learn and acquire information about the environment it's focused on. Its algorithms and processes can also use this new information to create up-to-date results and solutions. However, your AI agent will need a default set of knowledge - so it will be able to compute even if it doesn't acquire any new information. Overall, if you find that your AI agent's environment will change and vary over time (therefore affecting its processes), you may have your AI agent continuously learn about its environment and update its knowledge.

For example, your AI agent - as a self-driving vehicle - may be based on your local area. You know that residences may change owners over time and business/shops will be created or shut down. Also, traffic patterns can change throughout the day; there could be an accident at this street, or that street will have heavy gridlock during rush hour. Your AI agent can take note of all this information in order to get from place to place consistently and efficiently - by taking the better routes and even knowing where to go (or if a place for it to go to even exists).

Chapter 5: How to Create a Problem-Solving AI

==== ==== ==== ==== ====

Let's start developing our Search algorithm: an automatic problem solver. We'll have a general overview of it in Pseudocode. Then you'll get to code and run it on your own, with this book's primary programming language.

Abstract Search Algorithm

In its most basic procedure, a search algorithm will have a default condition and a goal condition. It will then evaluate each option it can take, starting from the default condition, step-by-step, until it eventually finds a full set of options to achieve the goal condition.

The General Frontier Search Algorithm:

The Frontier Search algorithm follows the same procedure as above. Given a start node, goal nodes, and an entire network, it will incrementally assess and explore pathways from the start node until it reaches the goal node.

The Frontier is simply a list of paths to be checked. The Frontier Search algorithm will keep adding paths to the Frontier until it either finds a solution or has explored the entire network

For example, this is just like giving a Search Algorithm a map of your local city, your current location, and a restaurant you're about to go to. That search algorithm will give you directions to get there.

The standard data structure to use a Search Algorithm with is a Network of interconnected Nodes. Each node contains an amount of data and a list of connected nodes:

```
// A Node has:
// - its data (any data type you want)
// - a set of connected nodes
class Node
        <some data type>: contents
        Array of Nodes: connected
```

The Frontier Search algorithm also uses Paths: a list of connected Nodes, with the first node as the starting point:

// A Path has:
// - a List of Nodes
class Path
*   Array of Paths: contents*

And finally, here is a generalized algorithm for Frontier Search:

INPUT:
- a Start Node (can be a class method in OOP)
- a graph network (only requires start node to have a network)
- a goal-checking procedure OR a solution query
OUTPUT:
- a Path from start to Goal (a List of Nodes)
- return FALSE or NULL if no paths found (wherever applicable)
EFFECT:
Frontier Search Algorithm: Returns a set of nodes that lead from the input Node to a solution node if found
PROCEDURE:
- frontier:= {new array of Nodes}
- create a new Path and put the Start node in it
- put the new Path into the frontier

While frontier is not empty {
*   - select and remove a Path <s0, s1,....,sk> from frontier;*
*   If node (sk) is a goal, return selected Path <s0, s1, ...,sk>;*

Else:
   For every connected node of end node sk:
      - Make a copy of the selected Path
      - Add connected node of sk onto
path copy
      - add copied Path <s0, s1,....,sk, s>
to frontier;
}
- indicate 'NO SOLUTION' if frontier empties

Further Search Strategies

This will be covered later on, but how the algorithm picks a Path from the Frontier will determine how the Search Algorithm works.

For now, let's apply the Frontier Search Algorithm.

RUBY 05a: Fundamental Frontier Search Algorithm

For the procedure below, select an IDE of your choice. You may also use online IDE's such as rextester.com, ideone.com, or codepad.org.

========================== ======

Below are the fundamental parts to a Frontier Search algorithm: the major algorithm and its data structures.

First, we start with the Data Structures. We only need to use two essential classes: a network node and a path. A Path contains is what the algorithm uses to store connected, sequenced nodes. It will also be the output type for the algorithm.

```
## A Path has:
## - A List of Nodes
## (can be modified to include more Methods/Fields)
class Path
  def initialize
    @contents = Array.new
  end

  def contents
    @contents
  end
end
```

Nodes will be the main data structure the Algorithm will operate through; the algorithm will search through the node and its connected nodes for a solution:

```
## A Node has:
## - Some Contents (Data type of your choice)
## - A List of other connected Nodes
## It can:
## - Search all its descendant nodes to find a solution
## (Our Search Algorithm as a Class Method)
class Node
  ## CONSTRUCTOR:
  def initialize(c)
    @contents = c
    @children = Array.new
  end
```

```ruby
def contents
  return @contents
end

def children
  return @children
end
end
```

Next are two Helper Functions you'll need. This first function helps the algorithm pick a path to check from a list:

```ruby
"""
## HELPER FUNCTION #1:
## INPUT: a List of Paths
## OUTPUT: a Single Path
## EFFECT: based on positioning of your choice:
## - Select & remove a path
## - return that path
## NOTE: you can modify the position assignment to
change the Search Strategy
"""
def pickPath(f)
  position = 0;
  ret = f.at(position);
  f.delete_at(position);
  for i in f
    puts i
  end
  return ret;
```

end

This second function checks if the last node in the path is a solution. One of the function inputs supplies the solution:

```
"""
## HELPER FUNCTION #2:
## INPUTs:
## - a Path
## - Node contents that have a solution
## <same data type as Node's container>
## OUTPUT: boolean
## EFFECT: outputs True if path contains a Goal
"""

def hasGoal(s, p)
```

```
p.contents.each do |i|
  if i.contents == s
    return true
    end
  end
  return false;
end
```

And finally, the Search Algorithm. The pseudocode is attached to the lines as comments so you can see how the procedure works. The algorithm also uses both helper functions described earlier.

```
"""
## MAIN ALGORITHM:
## INPUT:
## - a goal query
## <has same data type as node contents>
## - a Start Node
## (Start Node & its graph network accessed thru this
function)
## OUTPUT:
## - a Path from start to Goal (a List of Nodes)
## (multiple output types not acceptable in Ruby;
## empty Path as output if no solution found)
```

```
## EFFECT:
## Frontier Search Algorithm: Returns a set of
## nodes that lead from the input Node to a solution
node if found
"""

def search(query, start)
    ## - frontier:= {new array of Nodes}
    frontier = Array.new;

    ## - create a new Path and put the Start node in it
    p = Path.new;
    p.contents.push(start);

    ## - put the new Path into the frontier
    frontier.push(p);


    while not(frontier.empty?)
    ## - select and remove a Path <s0, s1,....,sk> from
frontier;
    ## (use helper function pickPath() )
    pick = pickPath(frontier);

    ## If node (sk) is a goal, return selected Path
    if hasGoal(query, pick)
        return pick;
    else
        ## For every connected node of end node sk:
        ## - Make a copy of the selected Path
        ## - Add connected node of sk onto path copy
        ## - add copied Path <s0, s1,....,sk, s> to
frontier;
        size = pick.contents.count
```

```
        last = pick.contents[size - 1]
        for n in last.children
          toAdd = Path.new
          toAdd.contents.concat pick.contents
          toAdd.contents.push(n)
          frontier.push(toAdd)
        end
      end
    end
    ## - indicate 'NO SOLUTION' if frontier empties
    ## (we'll output false if there's no solution)
    return false
  end
```

RUBY 05b: Using Frontier Search

For the procedure below, select an IDE of your choice. You may also use online IDE's such as rextester.com, ideone.com, or codepad.org.

========================== ======

Here, we implement the Frontier Search Algorithm step-by-step onto a simple node network:

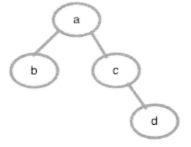

Each circle a, b, c, and d each represent interconnected nodes, which will only have their respective letters as contents.

We ask the algorithm if there is a path to a particular letter from a starting point.

The Search Algorithm would have a letter as an input. It would then check the nodes row-by-row until it either finds a suitable path from the input node to that letter - or notify you that a path couldn't be found.

So we now know what to expect. If we have, say ,'d' as the input, the algorithm is supposed to find it, and output the node path a->c->d. If we have 'g' or some other irrelevant letter as an input, the algorithm will say that it's not found.

Artificial Intelligence will heavily rely on Search Algorithms to come up with solutions and best decisions for its given situations. We will explore more about this later on.

Meanwhile, let's start building our algorithm.

Step 1: Understand & Create the Node Structure

First, we have to build the underlying data structure for our Network. Our Nodes contain the data type we want to use, as well as a list of its connected nodes. Since we're only using letters, our Node data type can be String.

Copy the class code below to your IDE. We'll build on from here.

```
## A Node has:
## - Some Contents (Data type of your choice)
## - A List of other connected Nodes
## It can:
## - Search all its descendant nodes to find a solution
## (Our Search Algorithm as a Class Method)
class Node
  ## CONSTRUCTOR:
  def initialize(c)
    @contents = c
    @children = Array.new
  end

  def contents
    return @contents
  end

  def children
    return @children
  end
end
```

Afterwards, we need the node network.

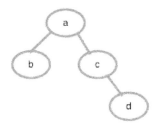

So it looks like 'd' is a connected to 'c', while 'b' and 'c' are connected to 'a'. We'll be re-creating this network in code.

Copy the code below and place it at the very bottom of your code:

```
## Creates & connects nodes a, b, c, d
$a = Node.new("a")
$b = Node.new("b")
$c = Node.new("c")
$d = Node.new("d")
$a.children.push($b)
$a.children.push($c)
$c.children.push($d)
```

Next, we need to design the Path.

Step 2: Create the Path Structure

The Path will contain an ordered list of Nodes. Each node will be connected to the ones next to it, while the first node in the Path is the Start node.

Copy the class code below to your IDE, just before where you put the Node class.

```
## A Path has:
## - A List of Nodes
## (can be modified to include more Methods/Fields)
class Path
  def initialize
    @contents = Array.new
  end

  def contents
    @contents
  end
end
```

Step 3: Start coding the Algorithm

(Before we move forward, it's highly recommended to review the Algorithm procedure in the past few chapters.)

Here, our search algorithm will be a standalone function. We can simply access it as a normal function, with a. a Node object as an input.

Since we are checking for letters, the search query will be a String - the same data type for the Node containers.

Place the Main Algorithm onto your code below, just after the Node Class you've created.

```
"""
## MAIN ALGORITHM:
## INPUT:
## - a goal query
## <has same data type as node contents>
##
## (Start Node & its graph network accessed thru this
method)
## OUTPUT:
## -  a Path from start to Goal (a List of Nodes)
```

```
## (multiple output types not acceptable in Ruby;
## empty Path as output if no solution found)
## EFFECT:
## Frontier Search Algorithm: Returns a set of
## nodes that lead from the input Node to a solution
node if found
"""

def search(query, start)
    ## - frontier:= {new array of Nodes}
    frontier = Array.new;

    ## - create a new Path and put the Start node in it
    p = Path.new;
    p.contents.push(start);

    ## - put the new Path into the frontier
    frontier.push(p);


    while not(frontier.empty?)
        ## - select and remove a Path <s0, s1,....,sk> from frontier;
        ## (use helper function pickPath() )
        pick = pickPath(frontier);

        ## If node (sk) is a goal, return selected Path
        if hasGoal(query, pick)
            return pick;
        else
            ## For every connected node of end node sk:
            ## - Make a copy of the selected Path
            ## - Add connected node of sk onto path copy
```

```
        ## - add copied Path <s0, s1,....,sk, s> to
frontier;
        size = pick.contents.count
        last = pick.contents[size - 1]
        for n in last.children
          toAdd = Path.new
          toAdd.contents.concat pick.contents
          toAdd.contents.push(n)
          frontier.push(toAdd)
        end
      end
    end
    ## - indicate 'NO SOLUTION' if frontier empties
    ## (we'll output false if there's no solution)
    return false
  end
```

It's considered a good programming practice to simplify what a function does. So instead of our algorithm function doing a lot of different things, it will call specialized helper functions to simplify the workload. This also makes it easier for programmers to check, edit, debug, and modify the code.

Step 4: Add the Frontier Path Picker Function

The path picking function for the Frontier Search algorithm is a customizable one in it own right, as modifying this function will affect the search strategy. We'll go over more search strategies later on. For now, just ensure that the function selects, removes, and outputs the path correctly.

Place this helper function somewhere in your code just before your Search Algorithm.

```
"""
## HELPER FUNCTION #1:
## INPUT: a List of Paths
## OUTPUT: a Single Path
## EFFECT: based on positioning of your choice:
## - Select & remove a path
## - return that path
```

NOTE: you can modify the position assignment to change the Search Strategy
"""

```
def pickPath(f)
  position = 0;
  ret = f.at(position);
  f.delete_at(position);
  for i in f
    puts i
  end
  return ret;
end
```

Step 5: Add the Goal-checking Function

This function helps the algorithm check a path for solutions. It will check all the nodes in a path to see if one of them has the contents the algorithm is looking for.

Since our query is a String, we'll use that data type as a function input. We'll also have a Path of Nodes as an input; we'll check whether or not there's a solution within these nodes.

Like the other helper function, place this one in your code just after where placed the Search Algorithm.

```
"""
## HELPER FUNCTION #2:
## INPUTs:
## - a Path
## - Node contents that have a solution
## <same data type as Node's container>
## OUTPUT: boolean
## EFFECT: outputs True if path contains a Goal
"""

def hasGoal(s, p)
p.contents.each do |i|
    if i.contents == s
      return true
      end
    end
```

```
    return false;
  end
```

Algorithm Testing

And finally, we test our algorithm. There's at least three major scenarios to think of: searching for the starting node's letter; searching for a letter further down the network; and searching for a letter that's not in the network. For each of these times, we want the algorithm to run through the scenario properly.

Insert this testing function in your code just after your Search Algorithm and Helper Functions:

```
def printer(p)
  if p == false
    return "NOTE: No Solution Found"
  else
  ## System.out.println("FOUND A SOLUTION!");
  s = "Solution Found! Path: "
    for i in p.contents
        s += i.contents + ", "
    end
  return s;
  end
end
```

Afterwards, we'll create a few paths generated from our Search Algorithm. Place the code at the very bottom of your code, just after the node network you've created.

```
## test search()
pa = search("a", $a);
pc = search("c", $a);
pd = search("d", $a);
pg = search("g", $a);
```

A search for the starting node's letter should output a Path with just the starting node. So Path 'pa' should have a path with only node 'a' in it.

If everything was done right, the code below should print out, "Solution Found! Path: a, ".

```
puts printer(pa)
```

A search for a letter somewhere down the network should output a Path with a sequenced list of Nodes. Paths 'pc' and 'pd' should have nodes 'a, c' and 'a, c, d' respectfully. If the codes below run, then they should print out their respective paths:

```
puts printer(pc)
puts printer(pd)
```

A search for a letter that isn't in the network should output an empty path, according to our current Search algorithm. So 'pg' should be an empty path. If you run the line of code below, it should notify you that a solution isn't found ('g' currently isn't in the network)

```
puts printer(pg)
```

And there we have it. A successfully operating Frontier Search   algorithm.

Chapter 6: Search Strategies

==== ==== ==== ==== ====

As mentioned earlier, the way the search algorithm picks a path from the frontier will determine the overall algorithm search strategy.

Now that we've developed our search algorithm, we can now modify it to suit any situation that arises.

Below are the four main ways that the search algorithm will pick a path to explore. The path picked from the frontier is either:

- the most recently added (Stack)

- the least recently added (Queue)

- the one with the least cost (Priority Queue)

- the one with the most value (Priority Queue)

We'll explore and analyze each strategy and implement them with our search algorithm.

Chapter 6.1: Depth-First Search

==== ==== ==== ==== ====

In Depth-First Search, the algorithm treats the Frontier Options as a Stack. Therefore, if the algorithm has a list of unexplored options it has yet to examine, it will explore the options and sub-options first.

Use Depth-First Search When:

- You expect long path lengths; in other words, the solutions will have long sets of options to get there

- You don't expect any nodes that are subnodes to each other)

- You don't have much space available

Don't use Depth-First Search When:

- The three looks fairly shallow. In other words, there aren't many levels of Option nodes in the tree

- If having the best possible solution is very important

Example: The Depth-First Search Algorithm

Consider the graph below. If all these nodes are placed on a to-do list for the algorithm, the last node added to the frontier would be processed first.

Node #1's options are added to the frontier: #2, #7, and #8. If Node #2 was added last, it would be processed first. So Nodes #3 and #6 would be added. If #3 was added last, then it would be processed first - so that means adding #4 and #5 to the frontier. The node depths are explored first - hence, why it's called DEPTH-FIRST search.

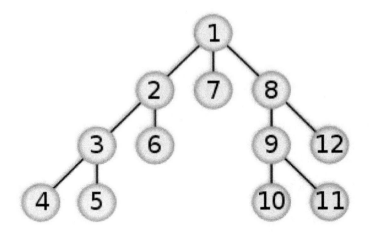

Algorithm Analysis: Depth-First Search

Is it Complete?

Sort of. Why? If there are any loops or cycles in the graph (meaning one of the end nodes link up to the beginning nodes, thus creating a loop) the algorithm might be stuck. It will keep exploring the end node, the beginning node, the path between them, the end node again, and so on and so on - probably in a sort of infinite loop.

On the other hand, if there are no loops or cycles in the node network, this algorithm is complete.

Is it Optimal?

No. If it gives off the first solution it encounters, it may not necessarily be the best one. There may be better solutions that have yet to be encountered before the algorithm gets to it.

What is its Time Complexity?

$O(b^m)$

Meaning, at the worst-case scenario, the algorithm will explore every node and reach the furthest tree depth. For example, if a node in a tree has up to 2 options and the entire tree can be up to 4 levels deep, the worst-case complexity will be 2x2x2x2 = 16 nodes possibly explored.

What is its Space Complexity?

$O(b*m)$

Meaning, at the worst-case scenario, a path for unexplored nodes will be stored in memory for every node explored.

The longest path possible is the furthest tree depth. Also, every node has a maximum amount of nodes it can explore.

For example, if a tree will have up to 2 options per node and the tree can be 4 levels deep, then the algorithm will store 2x4 = 8 units of memory

Chapter 6.2: Breadth-First Search

==== ==== ==== ==== ====

While Depth-first search has a Stack for the frontier, Breadth-first search has a Queue. In other words, if the algorithm has a list of options to explore, it will select the earliest added options and sub-options.

Use Breadth-First Search When:

• you don't have to worry about memory space

• you NEED a solution with the least amount of options chosen

• there are some options that can be explored that don't need depth

Don't use Breadth-First Search When:

• solutions tend to need a lot of options chosen (i.e. they're deep into the tree)

• you have a limited amount of space

• There's a high branching factor (nodes with many subnodes/options)

Example: The Breadth-First Search Algorithm

Consider the graph below. If all these nodes are placed on a to-do list for the algorithm, Node #1 would be processed first, then it's sub-nodes #8, #7, #2 would be added to the frontier in that order. Since Node #8 was entered first, it will be processed first. So Nodes #9 and #12 are added to the frontier. Then Node #7 is processed. Then Node #2, which adds Nodes #6 and #3 to the frontier. Then node #12 is processed, and so on. Overall, the algorithm will explore all nodes per level first - hence why it's called BREADTH-FIRST search.

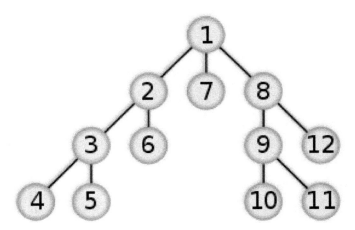

Algorithm Analysis: Breadth-First Search

Is it Complete?

Yes, as long as there's a limited number of subnodes. When there are nodes that are children to each other (for example: Node X is a sub-node to Node Y, and vice-versa), this would normally create a loop for Depth-first search. Node X would be added to the frontier, processed, then Node Y would be added and processed, then Node X is added, and so on - in an infinite loop. This won't happen in BFS. If Node X was added, all other nodes in the frontier would have been processed first.

However, if a tree has infinite subnodes per node, then BFS certainly won't stop. There will be just too many nodes to explore.

Hence, as long as there's a finite number of subnodes per node, you can guarantee that BFS will not loop indefinitely.

Is it Optimal?

Possibly. Because BFS is likely to find the solutions with the least number of options/steps, there is a chance the solution will be optimal.

What is its Time Complexity?

O(b^m)

Just like DFS, BFS will, at the worst-case scenario, explore every node and reach the furthest tree depth. For example, if a node in a tree has up to 3 options and the entire tree can be up to 4 levels deep, the worst-case complexity will be 3x3x3x3 = 81 nodes possibly explored.

What is its Space Complexity?

O(b^m)

At the worst-case scenario, BFS will explore every single node in the tree.

For example, if a tree will have up to 4 options per node and the tree can be 4 levels deep, then the algorithm will store 4^4 = 256 units of memory if it explores every node in that tree.

RUBY 06: Frontier Search as DFS and BFS

For the procedure below, select an IDE of your choice. You may also use online IDE's such as rextester.com, ideone.com, or codepad.org.

=========================== ======

When implementing Frontier Search, the algorithm will actually, by default, either be Depth-First Search or Breadth-First Search. This will depend on one key factor, as we will demonstrate below.

First, let's recall the path picker from earlier:

```
"""
## HELPER FUNCTION #1:
## INPUT: a List of Paths
## OUTPUT: a Single Path
## EFFECT: based on positioning of your choice:
## - Select & remove a path
## - return that path
## NOTE: you can modify the position assignment to
change the Search Strategy
"""

def pickPath(f)
  position = 0;
  ret = f.at(position);
  f.delete_at(position);
  for i in f
    puts i
```

```
    end
  return ret;
end
```

Note how the path picker works. The output path, chosen from the input array (the frontier), is based on an index position. That index is set on the first line of the procedure:

```
position = 0;
```

When items are entered into an array, they are sent to the end of the array like so:

[0: a][1: b][2: c]   <- inserting [d]

[0: a][1: b][2: c][3: d]

So setting the position to 0 means that the front (earliest) path on the frontier is selected. In other words, the path picker will treat the frontier as a queue. Therefore it will be BFS.

position = 0;

Before path picker call: [0: a][1: b][2: c][3: d]

After path picker call: [0: a][1: b][2: c]   Selected   For Processing: [d]

Otherwise, setting the position to the back (latest) path will need this line instead:

position = f.length - 1

The line above will set the position to the latest path added to the frontier. In other words, the path picker will treat the frontier as a stack. Therefore, it will be DFS.

position = f.length-1;

Before path picker call: [0: a][1: b][2: c][3: d]

After path picker call: [0: b][1: c][2: d]   Selected For Processing: [a]

Now, let's test everything we know so far on the below graph.

Bigger Search Graph:

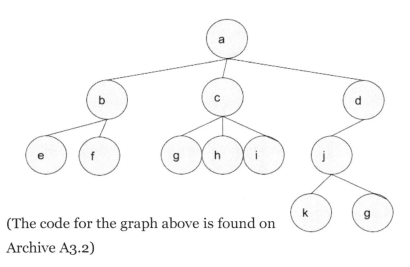

(The code for the graph above is found on Archive A3.2)

Place the code above into the bottom end of your code to create the graph.

We start with the completed Node and Path classes from the previous chapter. If you need to copy the Search Algorithm, Nodes, and Paths, see Archive A3.1.

We will then modify the pickPath() method to be either DFS and BFS.

Step 1:

We'll modify our pickPath() in the code below:

```
"""
## HELPER FUNCTION #1:(Modified)
"""
def pickPath(f)
     ## Breadth-First: uncomment line below to use
  ## position = 0
     ## Depth-First: uncomment line below to use
  ## position = f.length - 1;
  ret = f.at(position);
  f.delete_at(position);
  for i in f
     puts i
  end
  return ret;
end
```

Uncomment either of the lines above to set the position.

Step 2:

Next, we'll run and test the algorithm.

Before we do this, make sure you have the printer() function in your code. You can find this from either RUBY-02 or ARCHIVE A-01.

Moving on, simply add these two lines within your code, just after the code for creating the bigger graph:

```
pg = search("g", $a);
puts printer(pg)
```

There are two nodes that have "g" as their content. The algorithm will output either one as the solution depending on which search strategy you use.

If you set your pickPath() to DFS, the output lines should be:

Solution Found! Path: a, d, j, g,

Here's what happened after the algorithm processed Node a:

- the algorithm added Nodes b, c, and d into the frontier

- Node d was added most recently; so it'll be processed first

- Its subnode j is added

- Node j is added most recently; it'll be processed first

- Nodes k and g2 are added

- Node g2 is added most recently; it'll be processed first

- Node g2 is a goal. So a path with it and all its ancestor nodes is the solution path.

And if you look at the nodes carefully, you'll notice that the algorithm went "Depth-First":

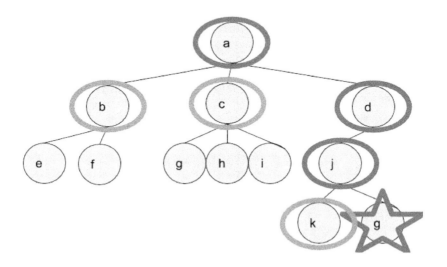

Otherwise, if you set it to BFS, the output lines should be:

Solution Found! Path: a, c, g,

Here's what happens after the algorithm processes Node a:

- the algorithm added Nodes b, c, and d into the frontier

- Node b is added first, so it's processed first

- So Nodes e and f are added to the frontier

- Now the earliest node is c, so it's then processed

- Nodes g1, h, and i are added

- Then Node d is processed, so Node j is added.

- Nodes e, f, and g1 are processed in that order, since they're now the oldest nodes in the frontier

- Node g1 is a goal, so a path including it and its ancestors is the solution path.

And if you look at the nodes carefully, you'll notice that the algorithm went "Breadth-First":

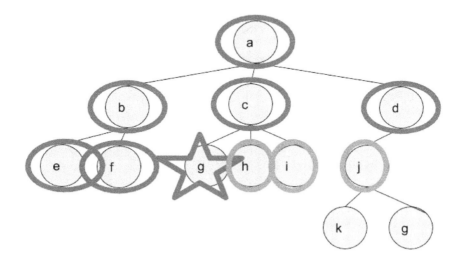

where the green-circled nodes have been processed already and the yellow-circled ones are in the frontier. They were supposed to be processed as well but the algorithm found a solution and finished instead.

Chapter 6.3: Lowest-Cost First Search

==== ==== ==== ==== ====

Sometimes, there can be costs between nodes and subnodes. For example, if a node had three subnodes, one of them would cost 10 to reach and the other two would cost 15.

So if the algorithm finds a solution, the path will have a total sum of all the costs required to reach the solution.

In this case, we want the solution that takes least overall cost to reach.

How it works:

The link between nodes and subnodes are called arcs. They can contain information vital for the algorithm to produce a viable, legal solution. For cost-based search algorithms, arcs will need costs between a node and a subnode.

[Node A] - - - -> arc A-B: cost=10 - - - ->[Node b]

Example: The Lowest-Cost-First Search Algorithm

Take note of the tree below. The red numbers indicate the cost to travel between nodes.

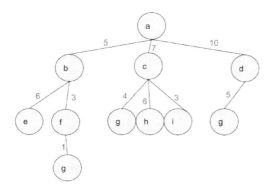

The algorithm will add Nodes B, C, and D to the frontier, as well as their respective costs, 5, 7, and 10. Which node will require the least cost to travel to? Node B. So Node B will be processed first, then Nodes E and F are added to the frontier, along with their respective total costs (Node E: 11 = 5+6, Node F: 8=3+5). Node C will be processed next, because it now has the lowest cost at 7. As you can see, the node that requires the least cost to reach is processed first.

Hence, why the algorithm is called LOWEST-COST FIRST.

Algorithm Analysis: Lowest-Cost-First Search

Is it Complete?

Yes, but there are certain conditions that need to be met. You can't have arc costs be zero or any negative numbers. If this happens, you risk having the algorithm loop and run forever.

So as long as the arc costs have real, non-negative values, you can expect the algorithm to either deliver a solution or tell you that there isn't any.

Is it Optimal?

Yes, and this is the algorithm variant's main strength. You can guarantee that LCFS will give you a solution and a path that took the lowest cost to reach, as long as the arc costs are, again, real and non-negative values.

Otherwise, the path costs will be distorted and the solution produced might not be the optimal one.

What is its Time Complexity?

O(b^m)

At the worst-case, the LCFS algorithm will process all nodes in the tree. For example, if a tree had up to 5 subnodes per node and 4 levels down, you're looking at 625 nodes to explore.

What is its Space Complexity?

O(b^m)

At the worst case, the LCFS algorithm will have every node in the tree stored into memory. So if you have a tree with 3 subnodes per node and 3 levels down, then you may have up to 27 nodes stored into memory.

Chapter 6.4: Heuristic Search

==== ==== ==== ==== ====

Another way to determine how to get the best path is to add heuristics to the arcs. The heuristic values can represent two things:

- A very low estimate of the total cost to reach a solution

- A value to maximize: the solution should have the highest value possible

In the first case, you can estimate the total cost to reach the nearest goal node from the start. It will be admissible as long as the cost isn't overestimated.

In the second case, it will be the opposite of LCFS - each node-to-subnode arc will then have a value and the algorithm will find a solution with the highest value possible.

How it works:

The link between nodes and subnodes are called arcs. They can contain information vital for the algorithm to produce a viable, legal solution. For cost-based search algorithms, arcs will need costs between a node and a subnode.

[Node A] - - - -> arc A-B: cost=10 - - - ->[Node b]
Example: Heuristic Search Algorithm

The tree below is the same one from LCFS, but now with added values to the arcs.

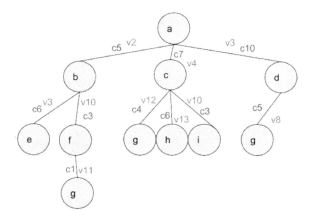

The Heuristic search algorithm will choose its nodes based on either the closest cost to the estimate or a maximum value. First, it adds Nodes b, c, and d to the frontier.

If, say, we estimate that the cost to get to Node g is 7, the algorithm will process Node c first because its cost is 7. So Nodes g, h, and i are added to the frontier, each with respective total costs 11 for g (4+7), 13 for h (6+7) and 10 for i (7+3). So Node b will then be processed next, because its cost (5) is currently closest to 7. Then its subnodes e (11 = 6+5) and f (8=5+3) are added. Node f is then processed, so a second Node g is added to the frontier, with a cost of (9=1+3+5). The recently added Node g has the closes cost to 7, so it's then processed. It is a viable optimal solution, since the other g-nodes have costs of 11 and 15 respectively.

On the other hand, we can also have the algorithm pick a solution that creates the highest value. If we want to pick the path to Node g with the highest value, here's what happens. Node c is processed first, because of its value (4). This adds Nodes g, h, and i with values 12, 13 and 10, respectively. Node h will then be processed next, but with no subnodes to add to the frontier. And once Node g is processed, i would be a viable solution, at a value of 12.

Algorithm Analysis: Heuristic Search

Is it Complete?

No, because there is a chance that the algorithm will be in an infinite loop once it cycles between two high-value nodes or two nodes closest to the estimate.

Is it Optimal?

Unfortunately no, but this is because the value-based or cost-based algorithms can be "greedy" at times. Meaning, the algorithm will only prefer the best possible node it has at the moment, but ignoring all other options. If deeper nodes have higher values, but the algorithm can't get to them because it processes other nodes instead, then the algorithm might produce less optimal solutions instead.

What is its Time & Space Complexity?

$O(b^m)$

At the worst case, a heuristic search will explore every node in a tree and have each node stored in memory.

RUBY QUICKSTART 01

To help you with the code, here is a complimentary quick start guide that helps you understand basic computer science, as well as fundamental programming tools.

For the code below, select an IDE of your choice. You may also use online IDE's such as rextester.com, ideone.com, or codepad.org.

=========================== ======

Part 1: Basic Data Types in Ruby

Booleans: They're either true or false. A LOT of computation will depend on booleans. In Ruby, they're either all uppercase (TRUE, FALSE) or all lowercase (true, false). Examples:

TRUE, FALSE
true, false

Strings: These are simply sequences of characters, including letters, numbers, and other symbols. They start and end with double quotation marks (" "). Examples:

" This is a String. "
" This 15 4 &^%$! 5tring too. "

Integers: They're exactly as they're defined - whole numbers without any fractions or decimals. Here are some examples:

12
143
19999932

Floats: also called floating-point numbers, they represent the opposite of Integers - they are numbers beyond the decimal point. In Ruby, you need to include at least one number before the decimal point - even 0 if you need to. Example:

0.12 # a Float in Ruby
.12 # NOT a Float in Ruby

Part 2: Ruby Variables

In Ruby, you can create variables in the following syntax:

(Variable Name) = (Initial Value)

Variables in Ruby need an initial value, but their data types can change to whatever data type you set it to.

Examples:

a = " This is a String. "

b = 122
c = TRUE
d = 0.1234

Part 3a: Ruby Classes, Composite Data, & Object Oriented Programming

Composite data is simply a data structure composed of smaller, more simple, and possibly diverse data types. A Class is a data structure that acts as "blueprints" and an Object is a "created copy" based on that class.

This is the essence of Object-Oriented Programming - one of the most popular programming styles out there. Classes are defined. Objects are made based on those classes. Get the objects to do stuff.

In Ruby, you can create classes in the following syntax:

class (Class Name)
        ## some code
end

You need the word 'end' at the end of your Ruby classes to indicate the end of the structure. The first line of the class, at the very least, needs the word 'class' followed by your class name

Example:

```
class House
        ## insert code here
end
```

To create a data object based on a certain class, follow this syntax:

(Variable Name) = (Class Name).new

You're essentially setting something as a data object based on some class. After the class name, you need to add a dot (.), followed by the word 'new'.

Example:

```
class House
        ## insert code here
end

h = House.new
```

To call a class object, simply refer to it:

Example:

```
h = House.new
varMyHouse = h
```

Part 3b: Ruby Class Variables

There are Three types of variables within Ruby Classes:

Global Variables: you can access these anywhere within your code. These have the dollar symbol ($) added in front of the variable names

Example:

```
class (Class Name)
        $GlobalVar = 0
end
```

Class Variables: these variables apply to EVERY object created, based on a particular class. Setting up data for a Class Variable affects all objects of that class. These have two at-signs (@@) added in front of the variable names

Example:

```
class (Class Name)
        @@ClassVar = " Hi there. "
end
```

Instance Variables: these variables apply to just one particular object created, based on a certain class. Setting up data for an Instance variable affects just that object only. These have one at-sign (@) added in front of the variable names

Example:

class (Class Name)
*   @InstanceVar = " Hows it Going. "*
end

Part 4a: Ruby Functions

Functions are merely actions and procedures carried out by the computer once they are called in the code.

To create a function in Ruby, follow this syntax:

def <Function Name>(input1, input2, ..., inputN)
write code here
* ## use this next line if the function outputs any data:*
return (variable name with data type, or any data)
end

You need the phrase 'def', followed by the function name, then any amount of inputs it has, within parentheses (()).

Examples:

returns an Integer, has no inputs:
def functionXYZ()
*   ##write code here*
*   return 12*
end

doesn't return data, has 3 inputs:

```
def functionABC(a, b, c)
        ##write code here
end
```

To call a function do the below as follows. If the function doesn't output data, follow this syntax - and make sure it's in its own line:

<Function Name>(input1, input2, ..., inputN)

If the function outputs some data, the syntax is similar as above. However, make sure the function is in a place where the output data type is expected:

(some variable) = <Function Name>(input1, input2, ..., inputN)

Examples:

No Output:
functionABC(a, b, c)

Outputs an Integer:
varInteger = functionABC(a, b, c)

Part 4b: Class Methods

In Object-Oriented Programming, Functions defined within classes are called Methods. Think of them as behaviours and actions that an object based on that class could do.

To create a method within a Ruby class, you're essentially making a function within a Ruby Class:

```
class ClassName:
        # other code here

        def <Method Name>( input1, input2, …, inputN)
        ## write code here
         ## use this next line if the function outputs any
data:
        ## return (variable name with data type, or any
data)
        end

end
```

Note: you need to place the proper ends on your Methods.

Examples:

```
class Dog
        ## some code

        def barkMethod()
        ## some code
        end

end
```

To call a Class Method, simply refer to an object (based on the class you want), followed by dot (.), then the method name:

(Variable as a Data Object).(Method Name)

If the Class Method returns a data type, remember to have it somewhere that expects that data type!

Example:

d = Dog.new
d.barkMethod()

Part 4c: Accessing Variables within Classes

You'll need to create Class Methods to access Class and Instance variables within your data classes.

This is simple; just define a class method that returns the class or instance variable. Preferably, name those class methods as the variable names

class ClassName:
        @@classVar

```
        @instanceVar
        # other code
        # ...
        def classVar()
                return @@classVar
        end
        def instanceVar()
                return @instanceVar
        end
        ## ...
end
```

Example:

```
class Car:
        @@numberOfWheels = 4
        @size = 12
        def numberOfWheels()
        return  @@numberOfWheels
        end
        def size()
        return @size = 12
        end
end
```

These work just the same way as regular Class methods do:

```
c = Car.new
x = c.numberOfWheels()
y = c.size()
```

Part 5: Arrays in Ruby

Arrays are a sequenced list of various data types. Those data types can be simple data or data objects.

To set up an array, follow this syntax:

(variable name) = Array.new()

Example:

a = Array.new()

You can also access individual items in a Ruby array, based on that item's position within the array. 0 is the first item; the array size minus one is the last item.

For example, you would get the first item of an array like so:

someArray[0]

And you would get the last item of an array like so:

an Array with room for 10 items:

someArray[9]

To process each item in an array, use these lines:

for x in (array name)

```
## every time you mention 'x' in this code,
## it will be applied to every item within the
array
end
```

For example, this would print out 1 to 5:

```
a = Array.new(5)
x = 1
for i in a
        i = x
        x += 1
        puts i
end
```

Part 6: Logic & Operators

There are three Basic Logic Operators: AND, OR. and NOT.

AND and OR are used to compare two or more statements that are either True or False. They are used in the form of (x AND y) or (x OR y)

AND is true if all items between it is true. OR is true if either one of its items is true.

NOT returns the opposite of a single statement it's set to; so 'NOT true' would be false and 'NOT False' would be true.

In Ruby, here are how the operators are:

AND operator: and

OR operator: or

NOT operator: not

Examples:

print false:
puts (true and false)
print true:
puts (true or false)
print false:
puts (not true)

Part 6: IF-ELSE Statements

The concept is simple: There's a boolean statement to check. If it's true, do the procedure after the IF line. If it's false, do the procedure after the ELSE line.

if (<insert something that would output a boolean>)
         ## code that happens if true
else
         ## code that happens if false
end

Note that the conditional procedures start after the IF and ELSE lines. They need the phrase 'end' to signify the end of the procedures.

an IF statement also doesn't need an ELSE statement; it can be by itself:

if (<insert something that would output a boolean>)
        ## code that happens if true
        end

Examples:

IF-ELSE together:
if (age > 20)
        drinkingAge = true
else
        drinkingAge = false
        end

IF-statement alone:
if (happy and knowIt)
        hands.clap()
        end

Appendix RUBY-A1a: Solving Schedule Problems

AI to Solve Scheduling Problems

Using Generate-and-test Algorithm

Copy and paste the code below to an IDE of your choice:

```
## ======= ====== ========

"""
# Appendix RUBY-A1
# Artificial Intelligence for solving Schedule Problems
#
# There's Four people: Anna, Betty, Cara, & Donna
# 1st Goal: Find out what times everyone is available to
meet together for Coffee
#
# Constraint 1: Anna has classes 11am - 1:50pm
# Constraint 2: Betty has classes noon - 3:50pm
# Constraint 3: Cara has work 7pm to 11pm
# Constraint 4: Donna has work 6pm to 10pm
"""
```

# Each person's waking hours, as a 24-hr clock, are represented by Integers
# For example: 15 would equate to 15:00, or 3am
# Everyone is generally free after 11am and before Midnight.
Anna = [9, 10, 11,12,13,14,15,16,17,18, 19, 20, 21, 22, 23]
Betty = [9, 10, 11,12,13,14,15,16,17,18, 19, 20, 21, 22, 23]
Cara = [9, 10, 11,12,13,14,15,16,17,18, 19, 20, 21, 22, 23]
Donna = [9, 10, 11,12,13,14,15,16,17,18, 19, 20, 21, 22, 23]

Goal 1: Have an hour of the day when EVERYONE is available to meet
INPUT: Four Integers, representing Hours
OUTPUT: Boolean
EFFECT: return True if all input hours are equal
def g1(a, b, c, d)
    return (a == b and b == c and c == d)
end

Constraint Functions
INPUT: an Integer, representing a friend's Hour
OUTPUT: Boolean
EFFECT: return True if the hour satisfies the time constraints

```
# Constraint 1: Anna has classes 11am - 1:50pm
def c1(a)
    return (a < 11 or a > 13)
end


# Constraint 2: Betty has classes noon - 3pm,
# then has dance practice until 4pm
def c2(b)
    return (b < 12 or b >= 16)
end


# Constraint 3: Cara has work 7pm to 11pm
def c3(c)
    return (c < 19 or c > 23)
end


# Constraint 4: Donna has volunteer hours from 6pm to 8pm,
# and work 8pm to 11pm
def c4(d)
    return (d < 18 or d > 22)
end
```

```
# Main Algorithm: Generate and Search
Anna.each do |v|
  Betty.each do |w|
    Cara.each do |x|
      Donna.each do |y|
        if g1(v, w, x, y) and c1(v) and c2(w) and c3(x)
and c4(y)
          ## === Solution Results are Here
          puts "Anna, Betty, Cara, and Donna can hang
out at: " + v.to_s + ":00"
          ## ===
        end
      end
    end
  end
end
## ======= ====== ========
```

Appendix RUBY-A1b: Solving Schedule Problems

AI to Solve Scheduling Problems

Using Generate-and-test Algorithm

Alternate Version: For Each Friend to schedule, Remove Unavailable Hours

Copy and paste the code below to an IDE of your choice:

```
## ======= ====== ========

"""
# Appendix RUBY-A1
# Artificial Intelligence for solving Schedule Problems
#
# There's Four people: Anna, Betty, Cara, & Donna
# 1st Goal: Find out what times everyone is available to
meet together for Coffee
#
# Constraint 1: Anna has classes 11am - 1:50pm
# Constraint 2: Betty has classes noon - 3:50pm
# Constraint 3: Cara has work 7pm to 11pm
# Constraint 4: Donna has work 6pm to 10pm
"""
```

Each person's waking hours, as a 24-hr clock, are represented by Integers

For example: 15 would equate to 15:00, or 3am

Everyone is generally free after 11am and before Midnight.

$Anna = [9, 10, 11,12,13,14,15,16,17,18, 19, 20, 21, 22, 23]

$Betty = [9, 10, 11,12,13,14,15,16,17,18, 19, 20, 21, 22, 23]

$Cara = [9, 10, 11,12,13,14,15,16,17,18, 19, 20, 21, 22, 23]

$Donna = [9, 10, 11,12,13,14,15,16,17,18, 19, 20, 21, 22, 23]

Goal 1: Have an hour of the day when EVERYONE is available to meet

INPUT: Four Integers, representing Hours

OUTPUT: Boolean

EFFECT: return True if all input hours are equal

def g1(a, b, c, d)

   return (a == b and b == c and c == d)

end

Constraint Functions

INPUT: an Integer, representing a friend's Hour

OUTPUT: Boolean

EFFECT: return True if the hour satisfies the time constraints

```ruby
# Constraint 1: Anna has classes 11am - 1:50pm
delList = []
  $Anna.each do |a|
    if (a >= 11 and a < 14)
      delList.push(a)
    end
  end
## (Delete ALL of Anna's unavailable hours)
delList.each do |z|
  $Anna.delete(z)
end


# Constraint 2: Betty has classes noon - 3pm,
# then has dance practice until 4pm
delList = []
$Betty.each do |b|
  if (b >= 12 and b < 16)
    delList.push(b)
  end
end
```

```
## (Delete ALL of Betty's unavailable hours)
delList.each do |z|
   $Betty.delete(z)
end


# Constraint 3: Cara has work 7pm to 11pm
delList = []
$Cara.each do |c|
   if (c >= 19 and c <= 23)
      delList.push(c)
   end
end
## (Delete ALL of Cara's unavailable hours)
delList.each do |z|
   $Cara.delete(z)
end
```

```
# Constraint 4: Donna has volunteer hours from 6pm to
8pm,
# and work 8pm to 11pm
delList = []
$Donna.each do |d|
  if (d >= 18 and d <= 22)
    delList.push(d)
  end
end
## (Delete ALL of Donna's unavailable hours)
delList.each do |z|
  $Donna.delete(z)
end


puts "Hours Free (after Unavailable Hours Removed):"
print "Anna: ";  $Anna.each do |a|; print a, ", "; end;
print "\n";
print "Betty: ";  $Betty.each do |a|; print a, ", "; end;
print "\n";
print "Cara: "; $Cara.each do |a|; print a, ", "; end; print
"\n";
print "Donna: "; $Donna.each do |a|; print a, ", "; end;
print "\n";
puts ""
```

```ruby
# Main Algorithm: Generate and Search
$Anna.each do |v|
  $Betty.each do |w|
    $Cara.each do |x|
      $Donna.each do |y|
        if g1(v, w, x, y)
          ## === Solution Results are Here
          puts "Anna, Betty, Cara, and Donna can hang
out at: " + v.to_s + ":00"
          ## ===
        end
      end
    end
  end
end
## ======= ====== ========
```

Appendix RUBY-A2a: Top Down Diagnosis

Top-Down Diagnosis of a Logic-Based System

Example code for the Water Flow System.

Note: In the code comments, you can find the original logic statements from the system.

Copy and paste the code below to an IDE of your choice.

Afterwards, call the Function topDownDiagnostic() and see what happens!

```
## ======= ====== ========
"""
## INPUTS:
## - a Boolean, for the Main Water Switch
## - a Boolean, for the Boiler Switch
## - three more Booleans, for each of taps D, E, and G
## OUTPUTS: none
## EFFECT: Run the Diagnostics to check if water can
flow through
## the washrooms, kitchen, and laundry washer
"""
def topDownDiagnostic (mainwaterStatus, boilerStatus,
dStatus, eStatus, gStatus)
    ## A <- MainWaterSwitch
    if (mainwaterStatus); tapA = true; end
    ## B <- A
```

```
if (tapA); tapB = true;
   puts "Tap A is on. " end
## C <- B
if (tapB); tapC = true;
   puts "Tap B is on. " end
## ToiletConnected <- D and C
if (dStatus and tapC); toiletConnected = true;
   puts "Taps D and C are on. " end
## ToiletFlushable <- ToiletConnected
if (toiletConnected); toiletFlushable = true;
   puts "Toilet is Flushable.";

else
   puts "Toilet Won't Flush.";
   end


## F and H <- BoilerSwitch
if (boilerStatus); tapF = true; tapH = true; end

## KitchenTap_Hot <- H
if (tapH); kitchenTap_Hot = true;
   puts "Tap H is on."
   puts "Hot water can flow through Kitchen Tap.";
else
   puts "There's no hot water from the Kitchen Tap.";
   end
## KitchenTap_Cold <- E and C
if (eStatus and tapC);
   puts "Cold water can flow through Kitchen Tap.";
else
   puts "There's no cold water from the Kitchen Tap.";
   end
## WashroomTap_Hot <- F and G
```

```
if (gStatus and tapF);
    puts "Tap F is on."
    puts "Hot water can flow through Washroom Tap.";
  else
    puts "There's no hot water from the Washroom
Tap.";
    end
  ## WashroomTap_Cold <- C
  if (tapC);
    puts "Cold water can flow through Washroom Tap.";
  else
    puts "There's no cold water from the Washroom
Tap.";
    end
  ## LaundryWasher_Hot <- H
  if (tapH);
    puts "The Laundry washer has hot water.";
  else
    puts "There's no hot water going into the Laundry
Washer.";
    end
  ## LaundryWasher_Cold <- E and C
  if (eStatus and tapC);
    puts "The Laundry washer has cold water.";
  else
    puts "There's no cold water going into the Laundry
Washer.";
    end
  ## BathTubTap_Hot <- F
  if (tapF);
    puts "Hot water can flow through the Bath Tub
Tap.";
  else
```

```
    puts "There's no hot water from the Bath Tub Tap.";
    end
## BathTubTap_Cold <- B
if (tapB);
    puts "Cold water can flow through the Bath Tub
Tap.";
else
    puts "There's no cold water from the Bath Tub Tap.";
    end
end
## ======= ====== ========
```

Appendix RUBY-A2b: Bottom Up Diagnosis

Bottom-Up Diagnosis of a Logic-Based System

Example code for the Water Flow System.

Note: In the code comments, you can find the original logic statements from the system.

Copy and paste the code below to an IDE of your choice.

Afterwards, toggle any global variable between true/false, then call the Function BottomUpDiagnostic() and see what happens!

```
## ======= ====== ========
"""
## Global variables for independent switches/taps
below.
## Switch them around between true/false,
## then run the Diagnostic on any water source.
"""
$mainWaterSwitch = true
$boilerSwitch = false
$tapD = true
$tapE = false
$tapG = true


"""
## INPUTS: Integers 1-5:
```

This determines which water source in the house the Diagnostic will check:
1: Toilet
2: Washroom Taps
3: Bath Tub Taps
4: Kitchen Taps
5: Washing Machine Water Feed
OUTPUTS: none
EFFECT: Run the Diagnostics to check if water can feed to the
Chosen water source in the house
"""

```
def botUpDiagnostic (mode)
    ## A <- MainWaterSwitch
    if ($mainWaterSwitch); tapA = true;
        puts "Main Water Switch is On." ;end
    ## B <- A
    if (tapA); tapB = true;
        puts "Tap A is on. " end
    ## C <- B
    if (tapB); tapC = true; puts "Tap B is on. " end


    if (mode == 1)
        ## ToiletConnected <- D and C
    if ($tapD and tapC); toiletConnected = true;
        puts "Tap C is on. ";
        puts "Tap D is on. "; end
    ## ToiletFlushable <- ToiletConnected
    if (toiletConnected); toiletFlushable = true;
        puts "Toilet is Flushable.";

    else
```

```
    puts "Toilet Won't Flush.";
    end
    return
end

## F and H <- BoilerSwitch
if ($boilerSwitch); tapF = true; tapH = true;
    puts "Boiler Switch is On."; end


if (mode == 2)
      ## WashroomTap_Hot <- F and G
if ($tapG and tapF);
    puts "Tap F is on."
    puts "Hot water can flow through Washroom Tap.";
else
    puts "There's no hot water from the Washroom
Tap.";
    end
    ## WashroomTap_Cold <- C
    if (tapC);
    puts "Tap C is on. ";
    puts "Cold water can flow through Washroom Tap.";
else
    puts "There's no cold water from the Washroom
Tap.";
    end
    return
end


if (mode == 3)
    ## BathTubTap_Hot <- F
```

```
    if (tapF);
        puts "Tap F is on."
        puts "Hot water can flow through the Bath Tub
Tap.";
    else
        puts "There's no hot water from the Bath Tub Tap.";
        end
    ## BathTubTap_ Cold <- B
    if (tapB);
        puts "Cold water can flow through the Bath Tub
Tap.";
    else
        puts "There's no cold water from the Bath Tub Tap.";
        end

        return
    end

    if (mode == 4)
        ## KitchenTap_ Hot <- H
    if (tapH); kitchenTap_ Hot = true;
        puts "Tap H is on."
        puts "Hot water can flow through Kitchen Tap.";
    else
        puts "There's no hot water from the Kitchen Tap.";
        end
    ## KitchenTap_ Cold <- E and C
    if ($tapE and tapC);
        puts "Tap C is on."
        puts "Tap E is on."
        puts "Cold water can flow through Kitchen Tap.";
    else
        puts "There's no cold water from the Kitchen Tap.";
```

```
      end

    return
  end

if (mode == 5)
  ## LaundryWasher_Hot <- H
  if (tapH);
    puts "Tap H is on."
    puts "The Laundry washer has hot water.";
  else
    puts "There's no hot water going into the Laundry
Washer.";
    end
  ## LaundryWasher_Cold <- E and C
  if ($tapE and tapC);
    puts "Tap C is on."
    puts "Tap E is on."
    puts "The Laundry washer has cold water.";
  else
    puts "There's no cold water going into the Laundry
Washer.";
    end

    return
  end

end
## ======= ====== ========
```

Archive RUBY A3.1: Frontier Search Algorithm

For the procedure below, select an IDE of your choice. You may also use online IDE's such as rextester.com, ideone.com, or codepad.org.

==========================

This is the default Frontier Search Algorithm used by most chapters throughout the book.

It is strongly recommended to view this only after you've finished building & successfully testing the algorithm already.

```ruby
class Node
  ## CONSTRUCTOR:
  def initialize(c)
    @contents = c
    @children = Array.new
  end

  def contents
    return @contents
  end

  def children
    return @children
  end
end
```

```
"""
## MAIN FRONTIER SEARCH ALGORITHM:
"""
def search(query, start)
    ## - frontier:= {new array of Nodes}
    frontier = Array.new;

    ## - create a new Path and put the Start node in it
    p = Path.new;
    p.contents.push(start);

    ## - put the new Path into the frontier
    frontier.push(p);
```

```
    while not(frontier.empty?)
        ## - select and remove a Path <so, s1,....,sk> from
frontier;
        ## (use helper function pickPath() )
        pick = pickPath(frontier);

        ## If node (sk) is a goal, return selected Path
        if hasGoal(query, pick)
           return pick;
        else
           ## For every connected node of end node sk:
           ## - Make a copy of the selected Path
           ## - Add connected node of sk onto path copy
           ##  - add  copied  Path  <so,  s1,....,sk,  s>  to
frontier;
           size = pick.contents.count
           last = pick.contents[size - 1]
           for n in last.children
              toAdd = Path.new
              toAdd.contents.concat pick.contents
              toAdd.contents.push(n)
              frontier.push(toAdd)
           end
        end
    end
    ## - indicate 'NO SOLUTION' if frontier empties
    ## (we'll output false if there's no solution)
    return false
  end


  """

  ## HELPER FUNCTION #1:
```

NOTE: you can modify the position assignment to change the Search Strategy
"""

```
def pickPath(f)
   position = 0;
   ret = f.at(position);
   f.delete_at(position);
   for i in f
      puts i
   end
   return ret;
end
```

```ruby
"""
## HELPER FUNCTION #2:
"""
def hasGoal(s, p)
p.contents.each do |i|
  if i.contents == s
    return true
    end
  end
  return false;
  end
## The Path Class:
class Path
  def initialize
    @contents = Array.new
  end

  def contents
    @contents
  end
end
```

Printer Function:

```
def printer(p)
  if p == false
      return "NOTE: No Solution Found"
  else
    ## System.out.println("FOUND A SOLUTION!");
    s = "Solution Found! Path: "
      for i in p.contents
          s += i.contents + ", "
      end
    return s;
    end
  end
```

Archive RUBY A3.2: Bigger Search Graph

For DFS & BFS, Chapter RUBY-06

For the procedure below, select an IDE of your choice. You may also use online IDE's such as rextester.com, ideone.com, or codepad.org.

========================= ======

Reference Image:

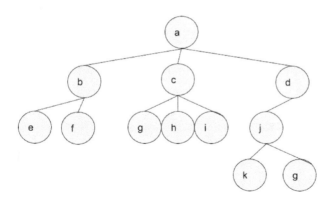

The code below is based on the default Node structure throughout the book.

```
$a = Node.new("a")
$b = Node.new("b")
$c = Node.new("c")
$d = Node.new("d")
          $e = Node.new("e")
          $f = Node.new("f")
          $g1 = Node.new("g")
          $h = Node.new("h")
          $i = Node.new("i")
          $j = Node.new("j")
          $k = Node.new("k")
          $g2 = Node.new("g")
$a.children.push($b)
$a.children.push($c)
$a.children.push($d)
$b.children.push($e)
$b.children.push($f)
$c.children.push($g1)
$c.children.push($h)
$c.children.push($i)
$d.children.push($j)
$j.children.push($k)
$j.children.push($g2)
```